GARFIELD

Yeah, Right!

JIM DAVIS

ℛℛ

RAVETTE PUBLISHING

First published in 2014
by Ravette Publishing Limited,
PO Box 876
Horsham
West Sussex RH12 9GH

www.ravettepublishing.tel

ISBN: 978-1-84161-388-8

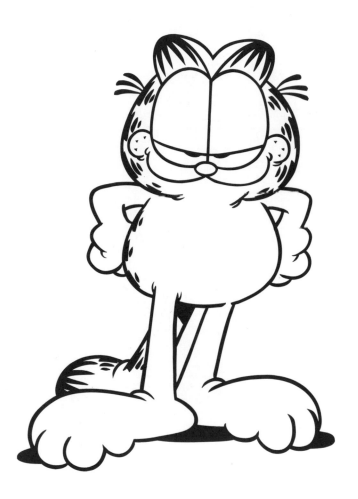

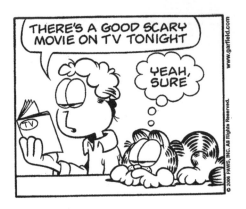

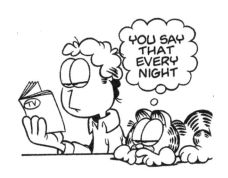

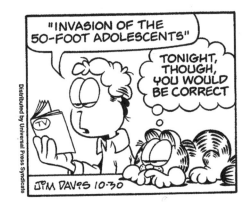

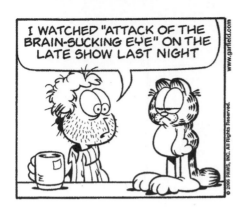

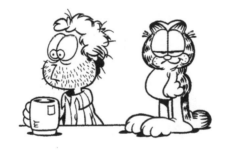

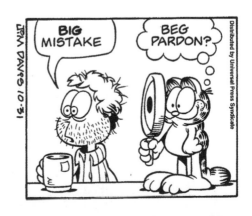

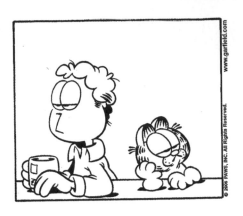

MEOW...MEOW...MEOW...MEOW

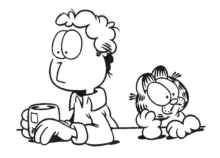

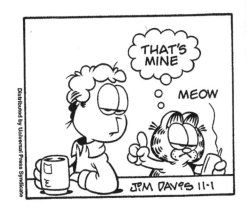

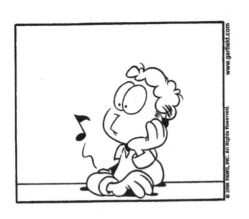

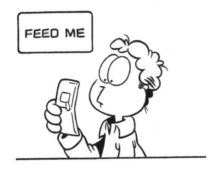

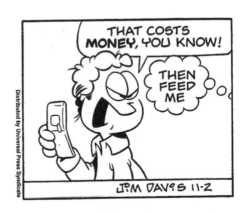

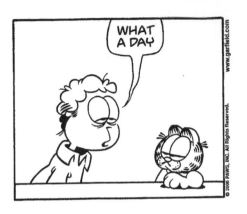

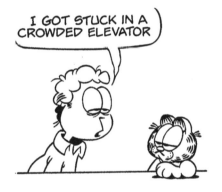

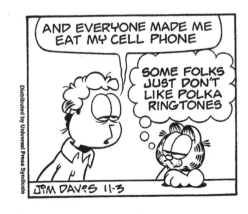

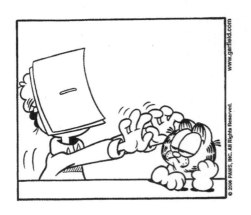

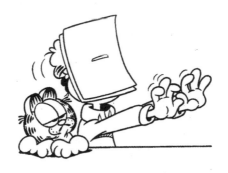

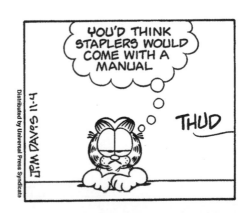

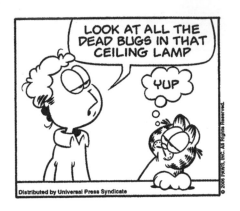

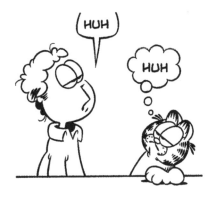

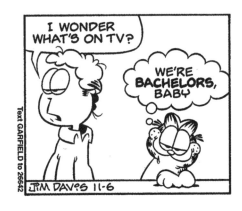

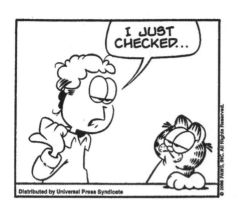

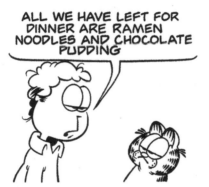

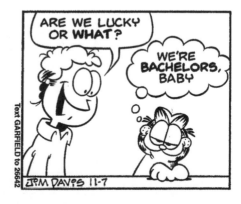

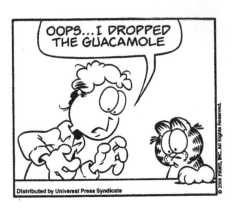

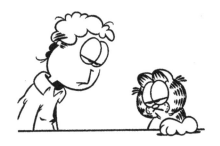

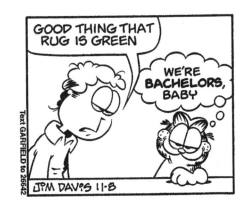

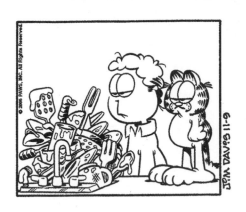

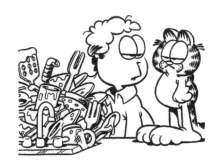

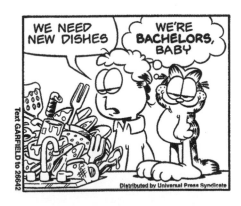

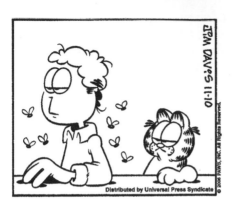

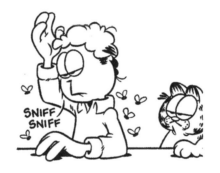

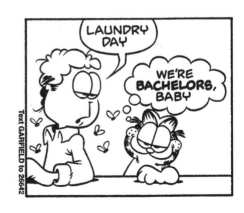

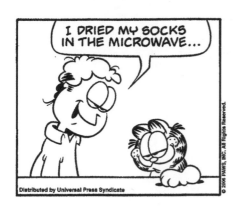

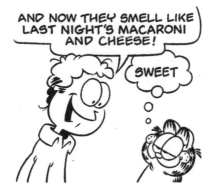

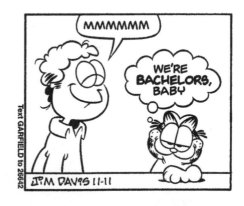

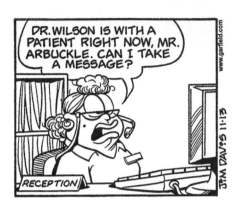

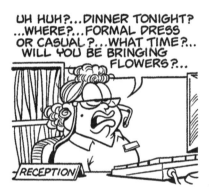

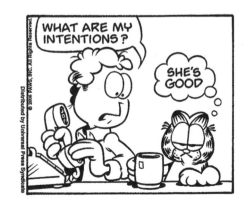

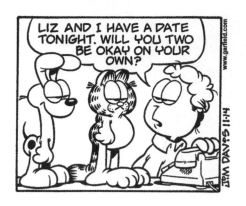

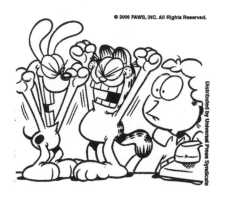

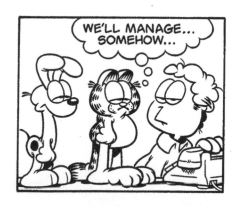

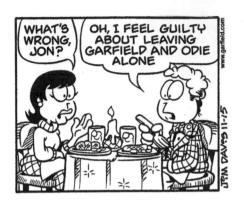

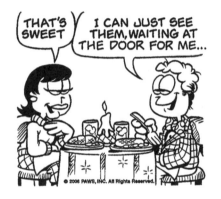

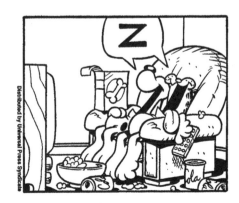

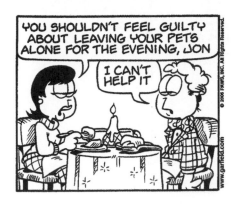

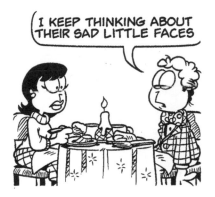

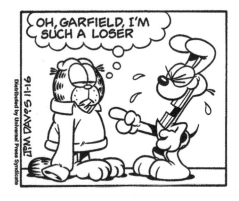

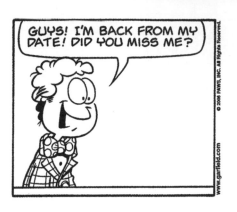

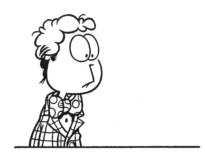

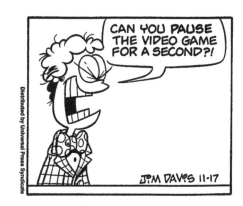

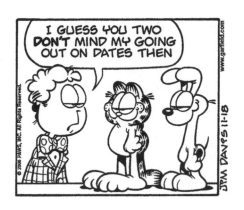

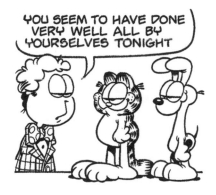

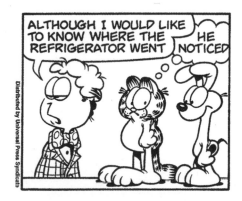

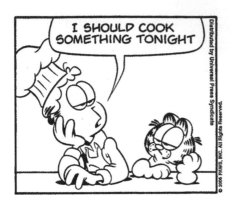

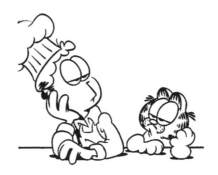

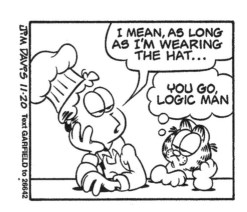

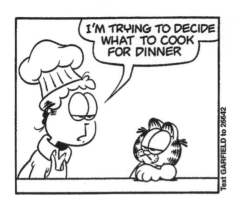

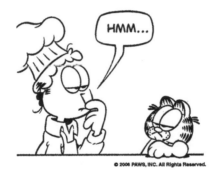

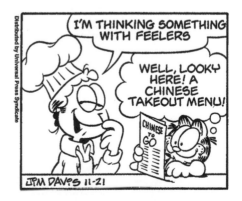

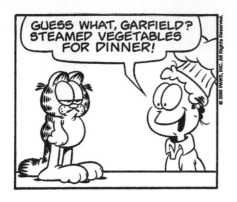

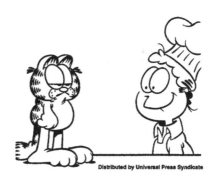

Distributed by Universal Press Syndicate

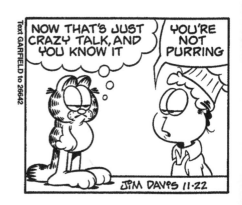

JIM DAVIS 11-22

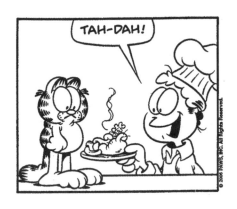

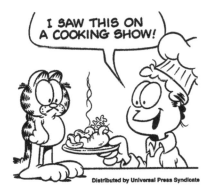

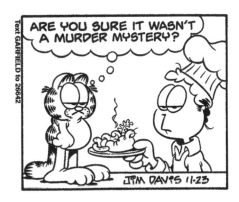

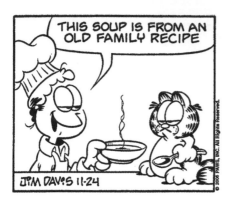

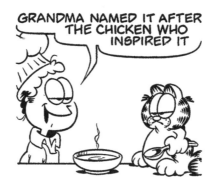

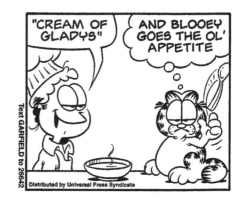

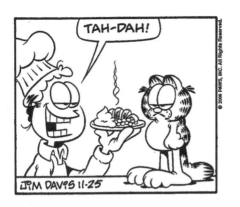

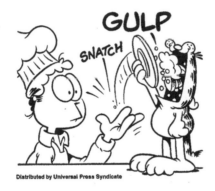

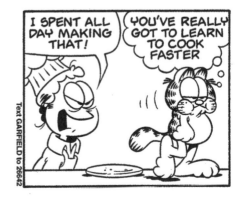

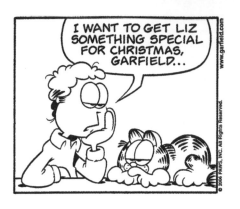

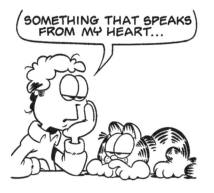

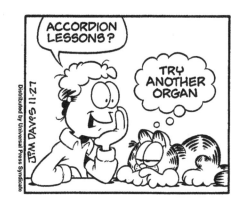

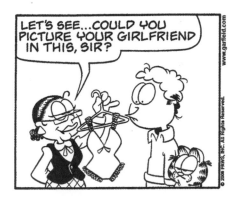

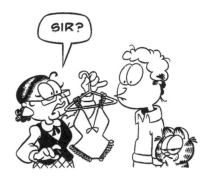

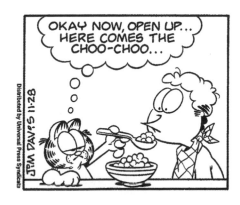

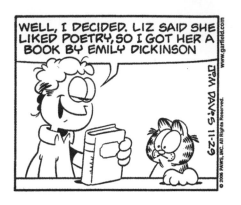

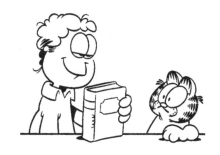

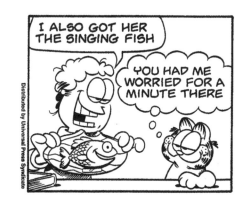

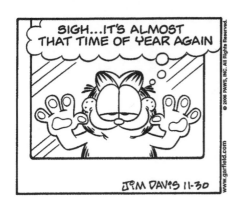

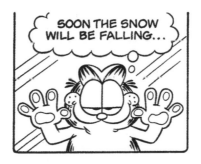

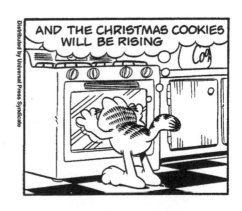

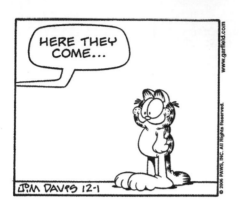

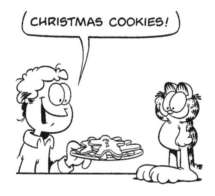

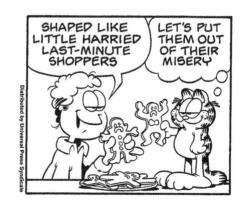

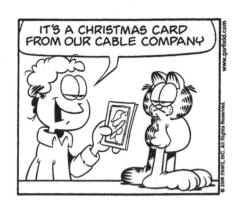

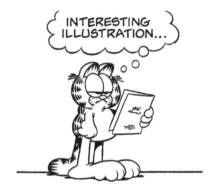

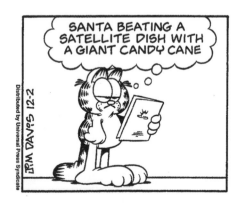

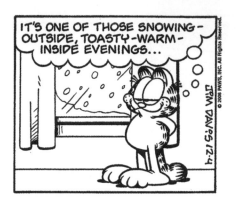

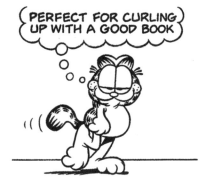

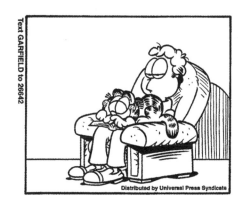

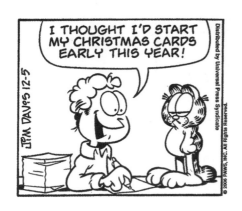

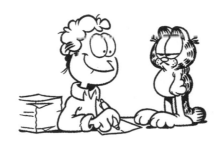

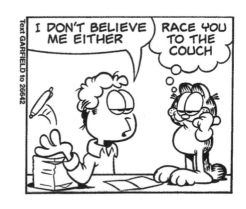

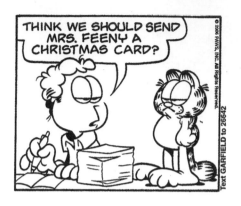

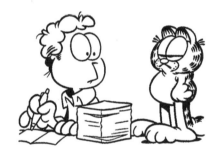

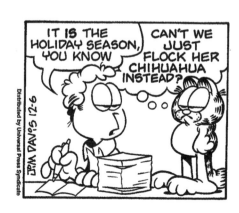

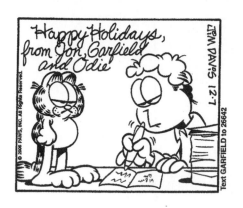

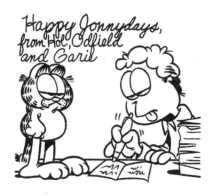

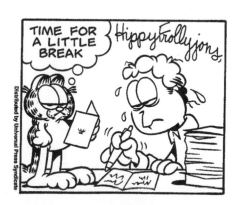

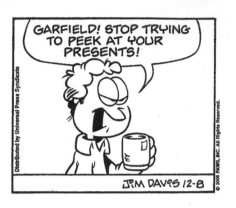

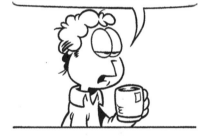

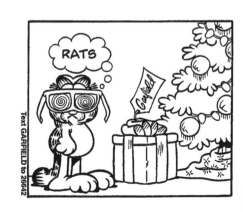

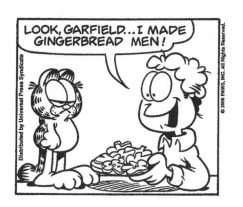

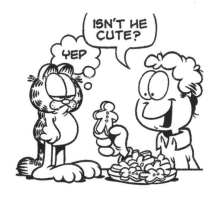

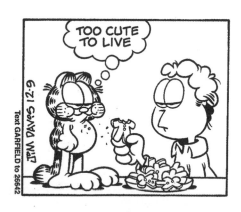

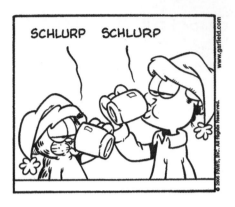

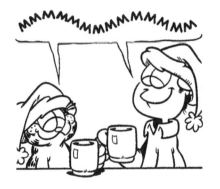

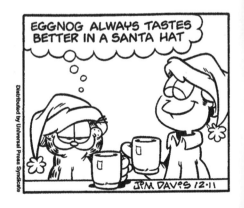

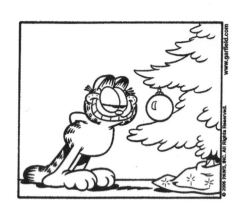

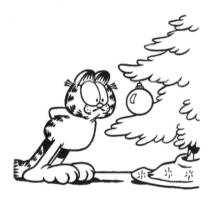

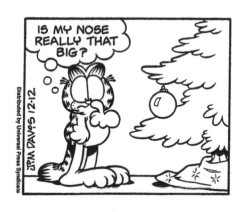

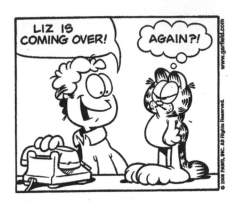

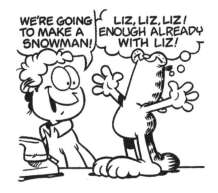

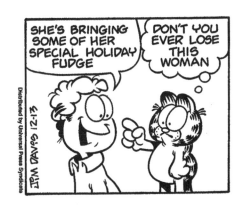

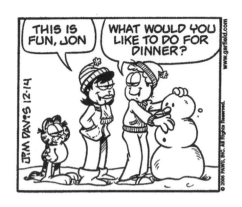

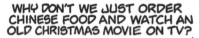

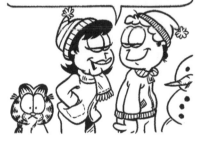

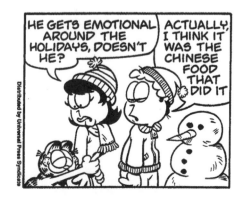

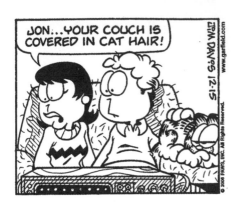

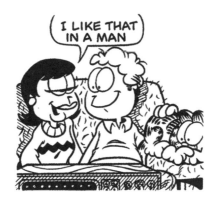

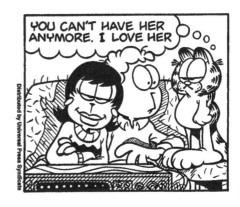

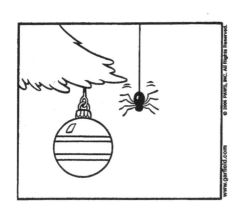

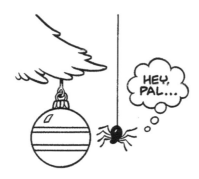

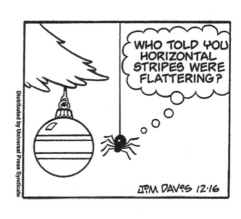

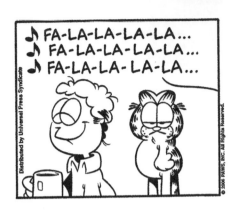

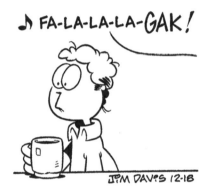

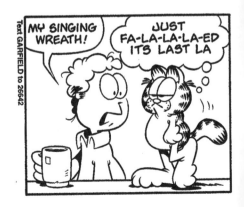

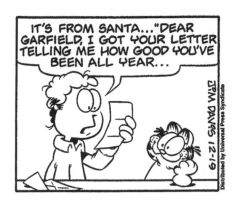

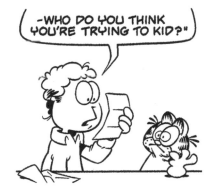

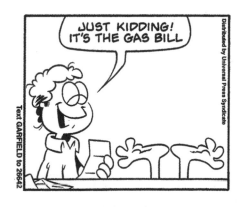

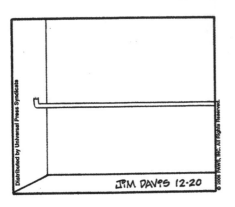

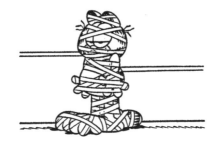

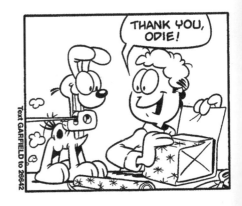

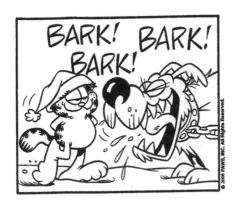

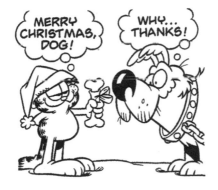

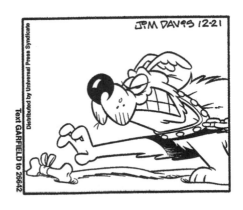

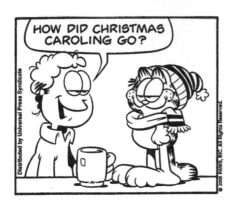

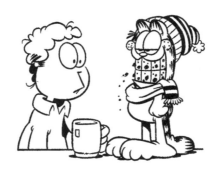

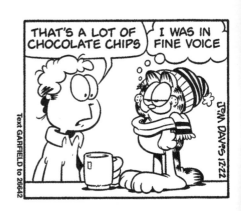

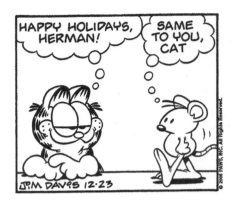

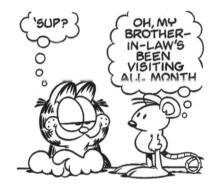

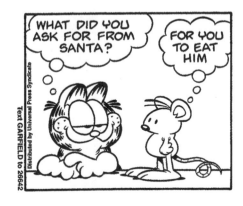

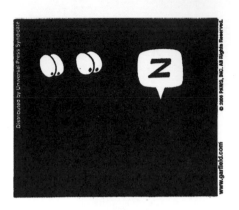

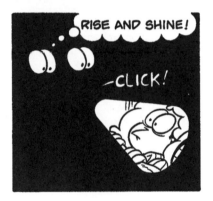

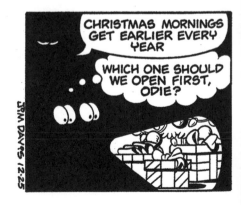

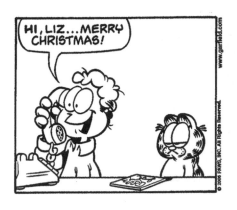

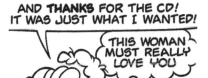

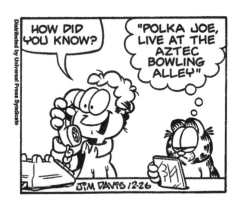

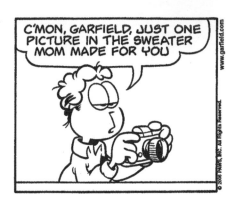

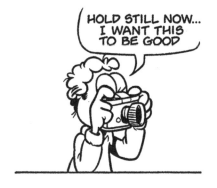

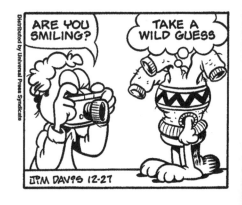

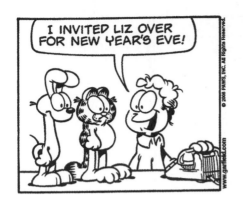

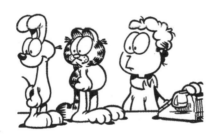

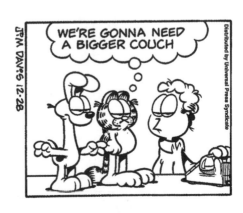

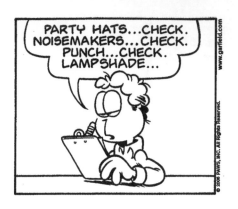

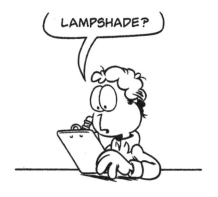

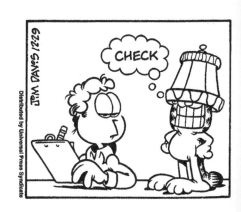

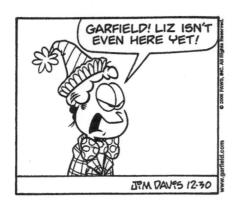

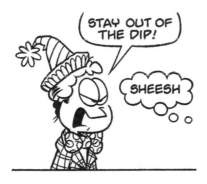

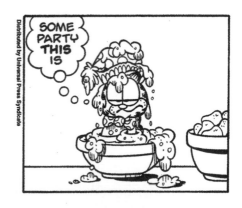

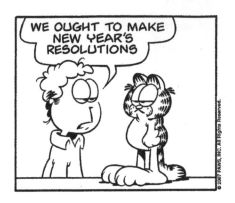

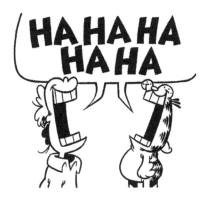

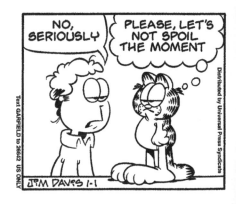

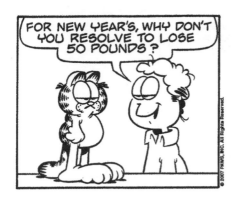

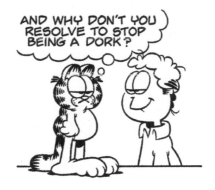

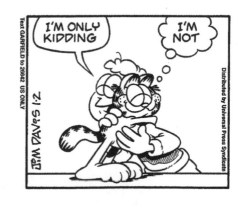

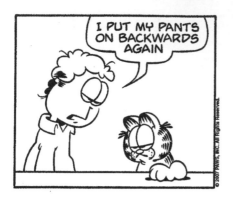

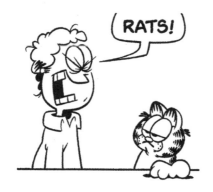

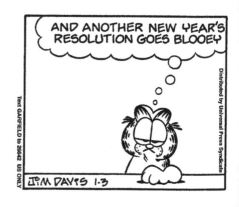

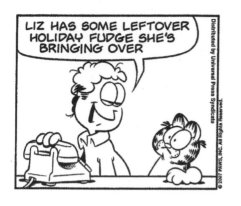

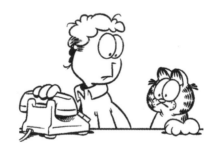

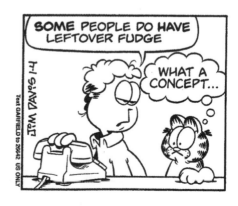

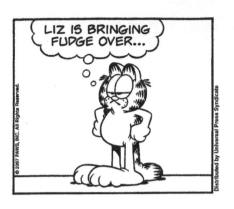

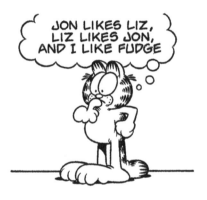

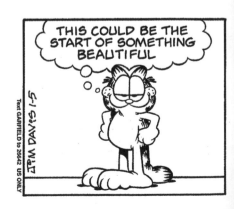

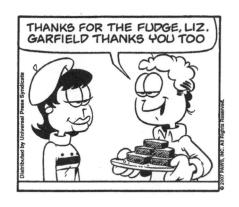

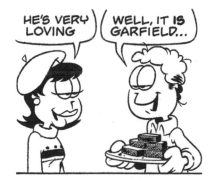

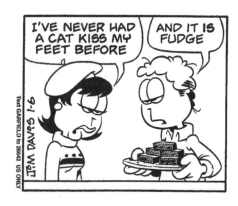

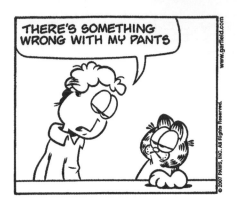

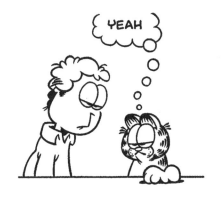

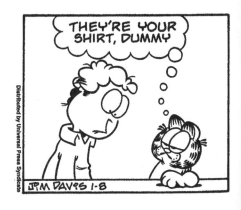

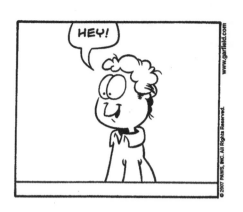

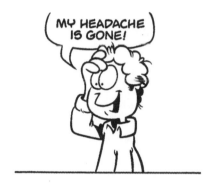

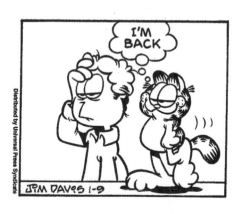

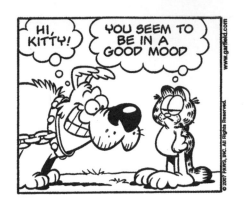

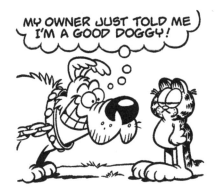

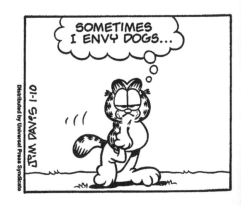

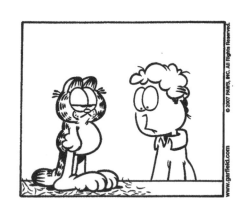

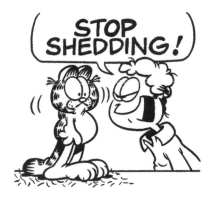

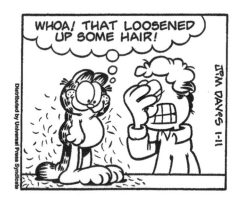

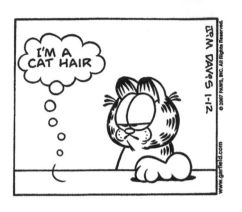

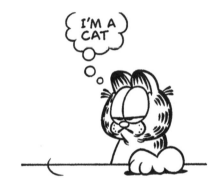

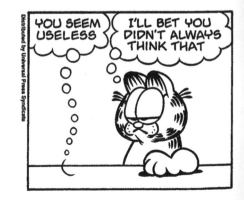

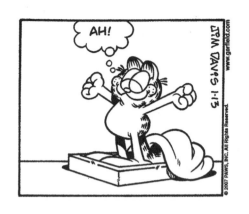

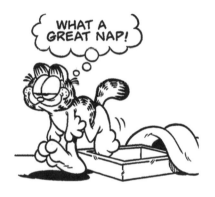

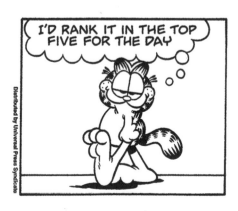

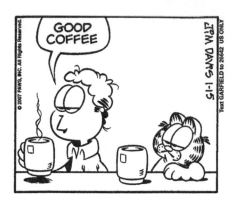

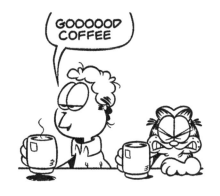

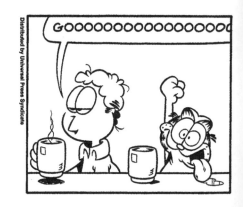

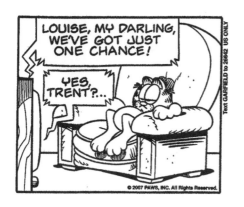

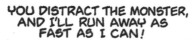

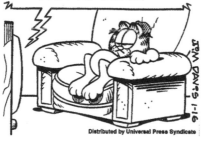

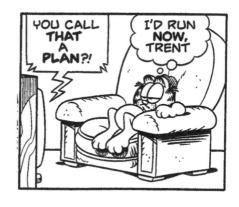

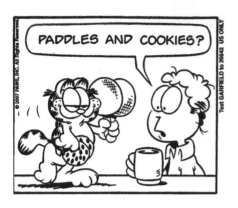

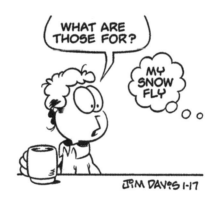

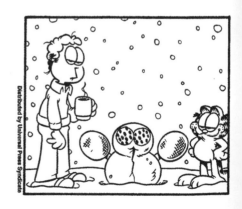

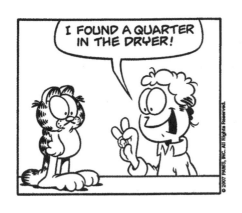

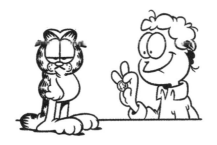

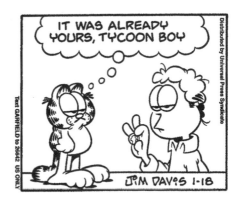

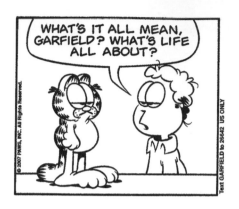

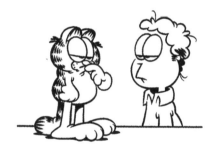

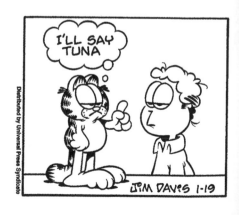

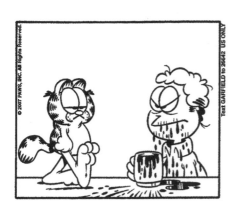

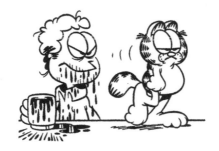

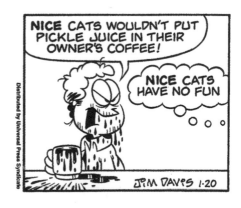

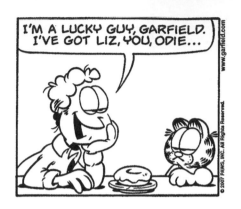

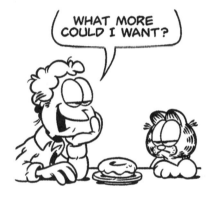

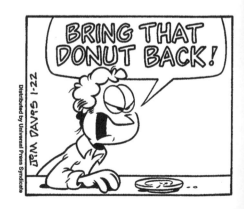

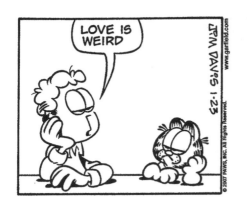

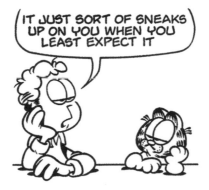

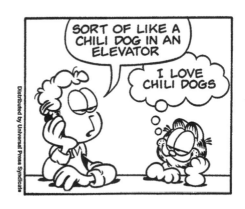

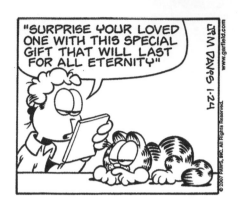

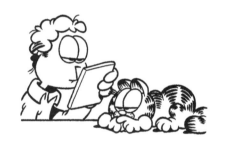

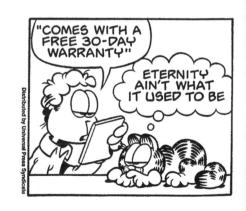

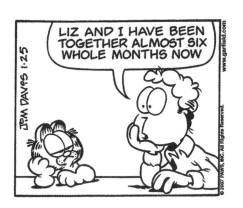

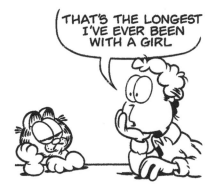

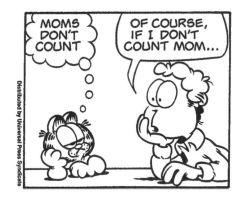

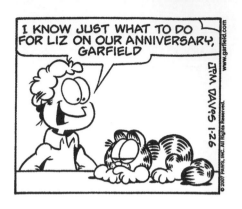

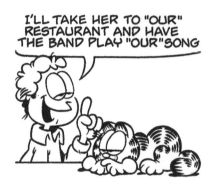

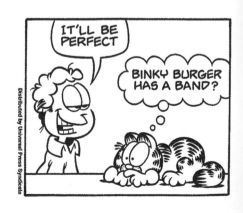

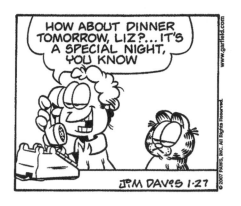

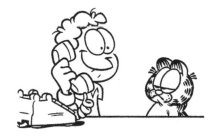

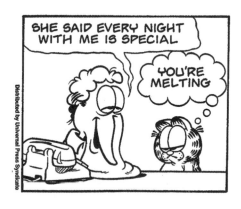

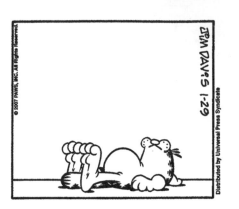

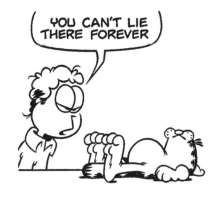

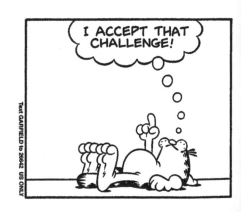

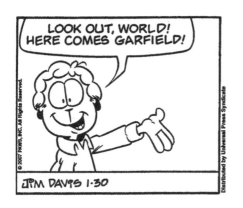

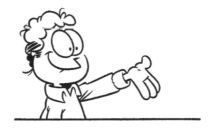

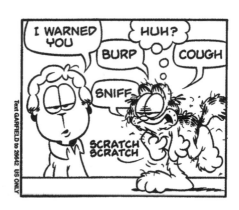

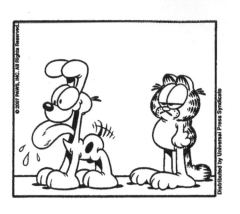

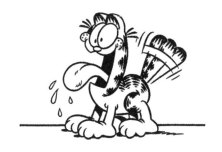

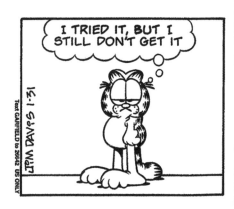

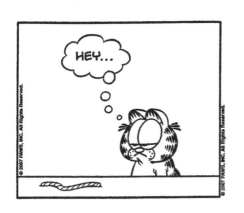
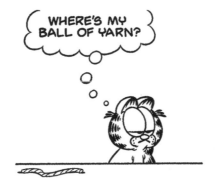
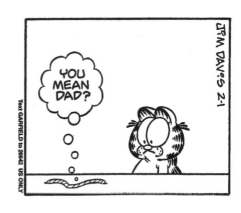

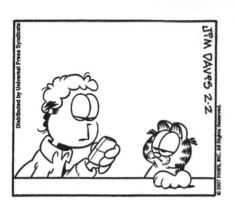

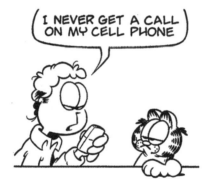

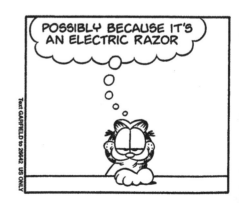

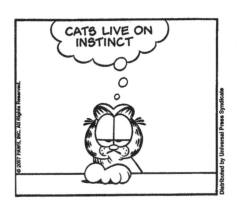

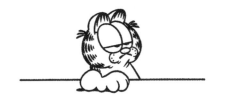

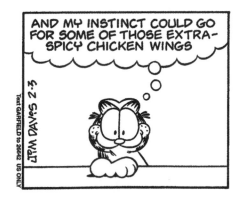

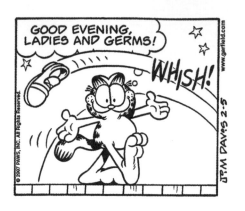

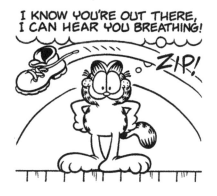

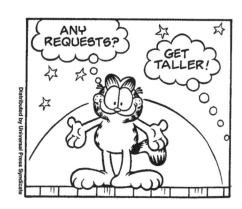

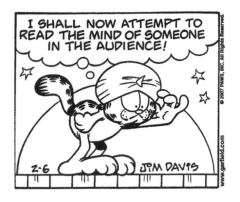

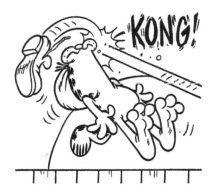

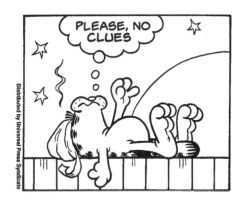

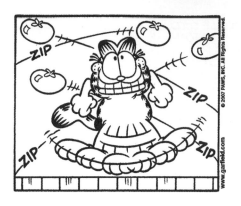

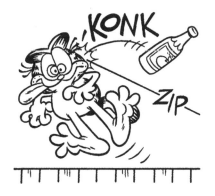

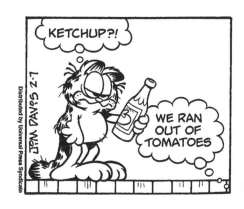

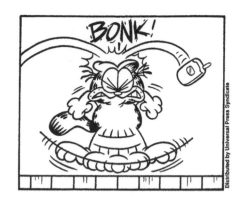

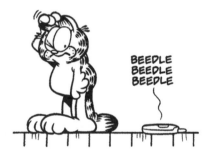

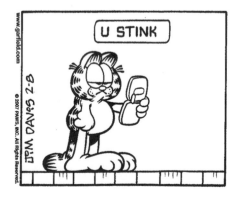

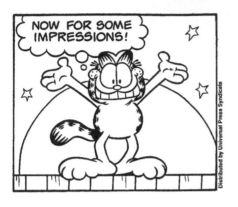

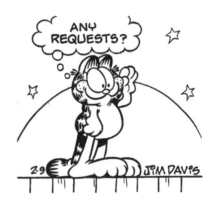

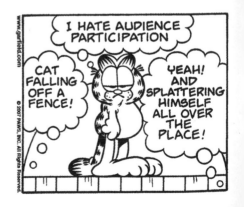

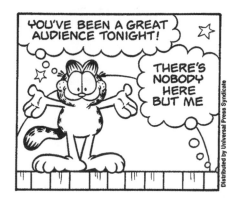
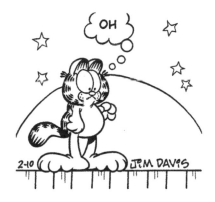
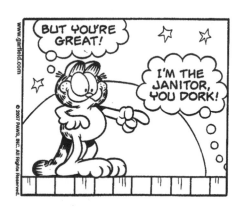

Garfield Pocket Books
(over six million copies sold)

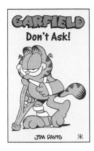 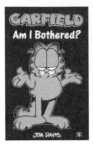 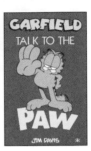

Pocket Books		Price	ISBN
Am I Bothered?		£3.99	978-1-84161-379-6
Don't Ask!		£3.99	978-1-84161-247-8
Feed Me!		£3.99	978-1-84161-242-3
Going for Gold		£3.99	978-1-84161-364-2
Gooooal!		£3.99	978-1-84161-329-1
Gotcha!		£3.50	978-1-84161-226-3
I Am What I Am!		£3.99	978-1-84161-243-0
I Don't Do Windows!	(new)	£3.99	978-1-84161-374-1
Kowabunga		£3.99	978-1-84161-246-1
Numero Uno		£3.99	978-1-84161-297-3
S.W.A.L.K.		£3.50	978-1-84161-225-6
Talk to the Paw		£3.99	978-1-84161-317-8
Time to Delegate		£3.99	978-1-84161-296-6
Wan2tlk?		£3.99	978-1-84161-264-5
Wassup?		£3.99	978-1-84161-355-0
Whatever		£3.99	978-1-84161-380-2
Your Point Is?		£3.99	978-1-84161-370-3

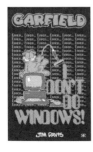 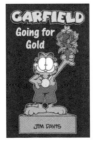 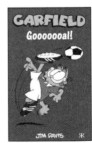

BOOKS AVAILABLE
Garfield Classic Collections
Each volume is a bind up of three Garfield Pocket Books

Classics	Price	ISBN
Volume One	£8.99	978-1-85304-970-5
Volume Two	£8.99	978-1-84161-381-9
Volume Three	£7.99	978-1-85304-996-5
Volume Four	£8.99	978-1-85304-997-2
Volume Five	£8.99	978-1-84161-022-1
Volume Six	£7.99	978-1-84161-023-8
Volume Seven	£7.99	978-1-84161-088-7
Volume Eight	£7.99	978-1-84161-089-4
Volume Nine	£8.99	978-1-84161-149-5
Volume Ten	£8.99	978-1-84161-150-1
Volume Eleven	£7.99	978-1-84161-175-4
Volume Twelve	£7.99	978-1-84161-176-1
Volume Thirteen	£8.99	978-1-84161-206-5
Volume Fourteen	£7.99	978-1-84161-207-2
Volume Fifteen	£5.99	978-1-84161-232-4
Volume Sixteen	£5.99	978-1-84161-233-1
Volume Seventeen	£7.99	978-1-84161-250-8
Volume Eighteen	£8.99	978-1-84161-382-6
Volume Nineteen	£6.99	978-1-84161-303-1
Volume Twenty	£6.99	978-1-84161-304-8
Volume Twenty One	£7.99	978-1-84161-359-8
Volume Twenty Two	£8.99	978-1-84161-378-9

All Garfield books are available at your local bookshop
or from the publisher at the address below.

Just send your order with your payment and name and address details to:-

Ravette Publishing Ltd
PO Box 876
Horsham
West Sussex RH12 9GH
(tel: 01403 711443 ... email: info@ravettepub.co.uk)
www.ravettepublishing.tel

Prices and availability are subject to change without notice.

Please enclose a cheque or postal order made payable to:
Ravette Publishing to the value of the cover price of the book/s
and allow the following for UK postage and packing:-

70p for the first book + 40p for each additional book.